D0640983

Rupert Murdoch

RUPERT

MURDOCH

NEWS CORPORATION MAGNATE

by Sue Vander Hook

Content Consultant:
Mary McIlrath, PhD
vice president, C&R Research

ABDO
Publishing Company

CREDITS

Published by ABDO Publishing Company, 8000 West 78th Street, Edina, Minnesota 55439. Copyright © 2011 by Abdo Consulting Group, Inc. International copyrights reserved in all countries. No part of this book may be reproduced in any form without written permission from the publisher. The Essential Library™ is a trademark and logo of ABDO Publishing Company.

Printed in the United States of America, North Mankato, Minnesota
112010
012011

♻ THIS BOOK CONTAINS AT LEAST 10% RECYCLED MATERIALS.

Editor: Rebecca Rowell
Copy Editor: David Johnstone
Interior Design and Production: Craig Hinton
Cover Design: Kazuko Collins

Library of Congress Cataloging-in-Publication Data
Vander Hook, Sue, 1949-
  Rupert Murdoch : news corporation magnate / by Sue Vander Hook.
       p. cm. -- (Essential lives)
  Includes bibliographical references.
  ISBN 978-1-61714-782-1
  1. Murdoch, Rupert, 1931- Juvenile literature. 2. Mass media--Australia--Biography. I. Title.
  P92.5.M87V35 2011
  070.92--dc22
  [B]
                                     2010042439

TABLE OF CONTENTS

Murdoch proudly became a US citizen on September 4, 1985.

BECOMING A US CITIZEN

On the morning of September 4, 1985, two limousines entered the underground parking lot of the US District Court in lower Manhattan, a neighborhood of New York City. Billionaire Rupert Murdoch lived in the borough.

He also worked there. His media conglomerate, News Corp., is headquartered in Manhattan's famed Rockefeller Center.

As Murdoch got out of one limousine, his wife, Anna, and their children got out of the other. The family was whisked into an elevator and up to the courtroom where Judge Shirley Wohl Kram presided. One hundred and eighty-five immigrants from all over the world, dressed in their best clothes and holding a copy of the oath of allegiance to the United States, were seated in the courtroom. The Murdochs sat in the jury box, apart from the other soon-to-be US citizens.

After Judge Kram gave a poignant speech on citizenship, Murdoch placed his hand on his chest, over his heart, and recited the pledge of allegiance to the US flag hanging in the courtroom. And with that, the 54-year-old Murdoch became a citizen of the United States. His wife and children did not do the same that day. As the *New York Post*—

"While other global media companies . . . possess power and influence comparable to that of News Corp, Murdoch often appears to stand alone among the ranks of modern media moguls . . . because, unlike those other companies, News Corp is clearly identified as a corporate arm that is strongly controlled by a single individual. It is therefore fair to say that his absolute control over News Corp, with its holdings of some of the world's most pervasive and influential media properties, makes Murdoch perhaps the single most powerful media magnate ever."[1]
—*David Gunzerath,*
Encyclopedia of Television

one of Murdoch's newspapers—snapped pictures, Murdoch and his family shook hands with the judge. Then, they left the courtroom the same way they had gone in.

The Decision

Murdoch had been living in the United States for more than a decade when he decided to become a US citizen. The media giant was born and raised in Australia and educated in England. He owned media companies around the world, including Australia, England, Hong Kong, and the United States. He had moved to Texas in the early 1970s

Murdoch's Offices

Murdoch manages his empire from his eighth-floor office in the heart of New York City. The building that houses Murdoch's company, News Corp., towers 45 stories in the midst of 19 high-rises called Rockefeller Center. The address is 1211 Avenue of the Americas, and it is home to some of the world's most powerful corporations. News Corp. is the building's largest tenant.

One wall in Murdoch's office contains a floor-to-ceiling world map. Lights illuminate the map from behind, highlighting the locations of hundreds of Murdoch's business ventures around the world. Countries lit up include Australia, Italy, India, the Netherlands, the Bahamas—even Fiji and Papua New Guinea. Major cities such as London, Los Angeles, and New York also glow.

Murdoch's office space includes three dining suites where he entertains and conducts business with a variety of guests. Each dining room has its own unique theme to match a specific medium Murdoch runs: newspaper, cinema, or television. Guests include corporate colleagues, competitors, politicians, royalty, and actors. The conversations that go on in Murdoch's office and dining rooms are private. Guests are confident that what they say there will not end up in one of Murdoch's newspapers the next morning.

following the purchase of his first US newspapers, San Antonio's *Express* and *News*. A very hands-on business owner, Murdoch wanted to play a major part in changing and developing his new acquisitions. He had admired US media for years and wanted to be a successful player there. The purchase of the San Antonio newspapers became the first of many Murdoch would make in the United States. The following decade, he owned major publications in Chicago and New York. But Murdoch wanted more.

After more than two decades in newspaper publishing, Murdoch had expanded into the medium of television in Australia, which was soon followed by the launch of the first cable television network in the United Kingdom. The billionaire newspaperman enjoyed his US newspapers and, by the 1980s, was eager to purchase television stations in the United States as well. However, federal laws prohibited noncitizens from owning US television stations. Determined to succeed, Murdoch made a decision: he would officially become an American.

Avenue of the Americas

The building that houses News Corp. at 1211 Avenue of the Americas, New York City, was built in 1973. It is part of Rockefeller Center, originally developed by US businessman John D. Rockefeller Jr. in the 1930s. Original buildings include Radio City Music Hall and the 70-story RCA Building, which is now the GE Building. Rockefeller Center was declared a national historic landmark in 1988.

Murdoch applied for US citizenship after moving to the United States to expand his US business holdings.

Murdoch had grown up fiercely proud to be Australian. As a young man, he openly proclaimed his love of his homeland. "I was very passionate about Australia," he recalled. "It was special, it was different."[2] However, he did not express passion or love of his birthplace when he became a US citizen. Rather, he noted only business: "I would very much like to remain an Australian citizen, because I have built what I consider a very big Australian company around the world."[3]

Some Australians were upset that their native son had abandoned his country. Even his wife was taken aback by the decision. Anna Murdoch said later,

"I was shocked. I never thought he'd do it. I realized then how strong his ambitious drive was."[4]

News of Murdoch's new status as a US citizen was printed in newspapers worldwide. The *New York Times* was not entirely kind to Murdoch. Reporter William Safire wrote, "Isn't it true that his main reason for becoming a citizen is simple greed and lust for power?"[5] Safire called him a "citizen of the world," a man with loyalties in New York, London, Sydney, and other cities around the globe.[6] "Americans should remind him," Safire wrote, "that allegiance means loyalty, sometimes passionate loyalty."[7]

Wanting More

While some questioned Murdoch's motives and his loyalty to the United States, one thing was clear: Murdoch was loyal to himself and his business. He had always been enthusiastic about his work. And he had thrived on journalism since he was a young boy, growing up the son of a father who was a journalist and a newspaper publisher. Murdoch had followed in his father's footsteps, but he wanted

Man of Power and Money

Murdoch's business savvy and extraordinary success have given him a great deal of power, influence, and money. In 2009, News Corp. reported earnings exceeding $30 million. Murdoch is said to have a personal net worth of $6.3 billion, ranking him, according to *Forbes*, number 117 on a list of the world's richest people in 2010. Among the world's media giants, however, he ranks first.

**Becoming
Americans Later**

Murdoch's wife, Anna, and children—Elisabeth, Lachlan, and James—did not become US citizens in September 1985. They did become official US citizens later.

more than his father ever had. "I was always reaching up to be bigger than just a little paper in Adelaide [his hometown]," he said.[8] And on that day in early September 1985, Murdoch showed his family and the world just how strongly he felt about having more than his father—and he himself—had. When asked why he had decided to become a US citizen, Murdoch answered simply, "Because I wanted to be, and I'm very happy and very gratified."[9]

Murdoch's desire for more—more power, more control, more influence, and potentially more wealth—was so great that he gave up citizenship to his beloved homeland. His wants as a businessman had, it seemed, outweighed his love of country. And though Murdoch's choice shocked his wife and many Australians, his decision was not surprising to others. The publishing giant had spent his decades-long career demonstrating his skill, determination, competitiveness, and sometimes ruthlessness in the newspaper business. His new status as US citizen would allow Murdoch to broaden and deepen his media empire and the US television and cable landscape, which was exactly what he wanted. —

Becoming a US citizen allowed Murdoch to acquire more media companies in the United States.

Melbourne, Australia

Young Rupert

Rupert Murdoch was born on March 11, 1931, in Melbourne, Australia. He was the second of four children and the first son of Keith and Elisabeth Murdoch. They named him Keith Rupert, but he would be called Rupert.

A Passion for the Press

Rupert was born into a family who valued freedom of the press. Rupert's paternal grandfather, the Reverend Patrick Murdoch, once said that freedom of the press was "probably the strongest foe of tyranny."[1] He claimed that "no autocrat [dictator] can tolerate the widespread dissemination among his people of a free discussion of his conduct."[2]

Rupert's father, Keith, also had a passion for the press and pursued a career in journalism. Keith's first job was working as a correspondent for an Australian newspaper in Sydney. Later, he became editor of a small news agency in London, England. There, he learned the newspaper business from English newspaper magnate Lord Northcliffe.

Keith returned to Australia, where he worked as a newspaper reporter and then took ownership of four newspapers. The newspapers were great successes with growing circulations. In the 1920s, Keith's company expanded to include more newspapers as well as magazines and a

Learning from the Best

Keith Murdoch learned the newspaper business from Alfred Harmsworth, Lord Northcliffe, a powerful British newspaper tycoon. Lord Northcliffe was famous for buying struggling newspapers and transforming them into profitable publications. His newspapers were entertaining and attracted a mass market. Lord Northcliffe dominated the British press, gaining political power and great influence over the masses.

radio station. It grew to be Australia's first media conglomerate. It was into this media atmosphere that Rupert was born.

Keith's flourishing media business was providing a healthy income that allowed a wealthy lifestyle. The family had two homes: a large house in the suburb of South Yarra and Cruden Farm, a 90-acre (36-ha) estate in the country, about 30 miles (48 km) south of Melbourne. The family enjoyed summers there in a large American-style colonial mansion. The estate included gardens, horse stables, and a tennis court. As a young boy, Rupert often went with his father to the offices of the Melbourne *Herald*. He called the life of a publisher "about the best life in the whole world."[3]

The Wedding Present

Keith Murdoch purchased Cruden Farm in 1928 as a wedding present for his wife.

Signs of the Entrepreneur to Come

When Rupert was seven years old, his father bought a sheep station, a large farm where sheep are raised for their wool and meat. Rupert and his older sister, Helen, rode horses and hunted for animals on the thousands of acres of rolling hills. They also

Keith Murdoch, left, with Press Chief at the Ministry of Information Mr. Brebner in 1941

hunted and trapped water rats. Rupert sold each skin for sixpence, or six pennies, and gave Helen one penny per skin, keeping most of the money for himself. He also went around town selling bags of rabbit manure that he gathered at Cruden Farm and on the beach at nearby Davies Bay. Helen later said,

> *I always say that Rupert got his start in life from rabbits, and manure. I never saw any of the money. Rupert did. He spent it on gambling at school.*[4]

Rupert's interest in gambling was probably inherited from his maternal grandfather, Rupert Greene. He was a colorful character who enjoyed drinking and gambling. Rupert later shared,

> *My father thought he [grandpa Rupert Greene] was a wild, drinking, gambling man. They all got on for the sake of family life, but it was one of my father's nightmares that I'd turn out like my grandfather, which I probably did a bit.*[5]

Rupert seemed to be a mixture of both grandfathers: passionate for freedom of the press and willing to take risks.

Boarding School

When Rupert was ten years old, he was sent to Geelong Grammar School, Australia's most elite boarding school. He did not enjoy his years there. When he returned home for the holidays, his mother would not allow him to stay in the house. Rupert lived in a hut in the garden that had no heat, electricity, or running water. Rupert's mother believed this would strengthen her son's character.

At school, Rupert was bullied a lot and became a loner. He believed he was picked on because of his father's position as a powerful newspaper tycoon.

The conservative slant of his father's publications brought ridicule from Rupert's more radical classmates. Rupert found out that people who manage the news are rarely popular.

College Life

In 1950, Rupert was admitted to Worcester College, part of Oxford University in Great Britain. He studied politics, economics, and philosophy. According to one of his biographers, Rupert was "a normal, red-blooded college student who had many friends, chased girls, went on the usual drinking binges, engaged in slapdash horseplay, tried at sports, and never had enough money, no doubt due to his gambling."[6]

Rupert became friends with some of his British history professors, but he did not think highly of England or the English way of doing things. He felt the country was not competitive and the people were satisfied with the way things were. He said of the English, "They distrust money.

Geelong Grammar School

In 2010, Geelong Grammar School was Australia's largest coeducational boarding school, with five campuses and approximately 1,500 students. Eight hundred of them live at the school. Geelong was established in 1855 by the Church of England. The school's most notable alumni include Rupert Murdoch, Prince Charles of Wales, and John Gorton, who was prime minister of Australia from 1968 to 1971.

They despise business. They create the social and psychological currents which have done so much damage to Britain and its willingness to change."[7] He did not hesitate to proclaim his devotion to Australia, and he resented other Aussies who did not share his patriotism.

Keith Arthur Murdoch

Keith Arthur Murdoch, Rupert's father, was born in Australia in 1885. His parents had migrated there from Scotland. A severe stuttering problem made Keith an extremely shy child who avoided talking to other people. He traveled to England to study at the London School of Economics and to find treatment for his speech problem. The experience did not go as well as Keith had hoped. He did not get a job on London's famous Fleet Street, and his stuttering did not improve.

Keith returned to Melbourne in 1910. In 1912, the 27-year-old became a political correspondent for the popular newspaper, the *Sydney Sun.* Two years later, he became news editor for the *Sydney World.*

World War I broke out in 1914. Keith worked as a war correspondent. He wrote dramatic and sometimes opinionated stories. After the war, which ended in 1918, Keith became managing editor of the Melbourne *Herald.*

Keith Murdoch was also a strong supporter of art, and he organized art exhibitions and revived art galleries.

Letters to His Father

While Rupert was at Oxford, he and his father exchanged many letters. Keith closely examined his son's letters to determine whether Rupert was qualified to be a journalist. Rupert's poorly written letters disappointed him, and clearly written ones delighted him.

While he was in England, Rupert made friends with Rohan Rivett, one of Keith's news correspondents. Rivett worked in the London office of the Melbourne *Herald*. The Rivetts became like a second family to Rupert, and Rupert often visited the Rivetts' London home. Rivett was impressed with Rupert and often wrote to Keith, updating him on his son's progress. In one letter, he wrote, "I am inclined to prophesy that he will make his first million with fantastic ease."[8]

Keith had been in poor health for several years prior to Rupert's move to England. In 1951, he began putting his affairs together to make sure his family was provided for. He sold his shares in some of his newspapers to buy more shares in others, such as the Adelaide *News*. He was becoming more optimistic that Rupert would be able to take over his business affairs.

In October 1952, Keith read a particularly well-written letter from Rupert. Keith told his wife, Elisabeth, that Rupert "got it!"[9] Two days later, on October 4, Keith Murdoch died in his sleep at the age of 67. Twenty-one-year-old Rupert inherited his father's media business. And his father's estate taxes would take most of the inheritance. Rupert would begin his journalism career with one small newspaper—the Adelaide *News*. It was a small beginning that would soon lead to greater media success. —

"I desire that my said son Keith Rupert Murdoch should have the great opportunity of spending a useful altruistic and full life in newspaper and broadcasting activities and of ultimately occupying a position of high responsibility in that field with the support of my trustees if they consider him worthy of that support."[10]

—*Keith Murdoch's will, 1948*

Rupert was attending prestigious Oxford University when his father died.

His father's death set Murdoch on a path of success in the newspaper business.

BEGINNINGS OF
AN EMPIRE

Murdoch did not attend his father's funeral. He had not yet returned home from Oxford University. Murdoch soon learned his father's business was in a state of confusion. The wealth Keith had accumulated was tied up in his newspapers, which were all in financial trouble.

Trustees of his father's estate suggested the newspapers be sold. The sales would pay for estate taxes as well as Keith's personal debts. Keith's widow, Elisabeth, agreed to sell the family's share of the Queensland newspapers, but the family kept its half share in the Adelaide *News*. When Murdoch returned to Australia, he took over as publisher of the *News*. Rohan Rivett was the editor.

The Adelaide *News*

After he inherited the Adelaide *News* from his father in 1952, Murdoch held on to the publication for 35 years. Murdoch sold the publication in 1987. The *News* stopped publication in 1992.

FIERCE COMPETITION

Owners of the *Advertiser*, a rival newspaper in Adelaide, offered to buy the *News*. When Murdoch refused, the *Advertiser* tried to run him out of business. Murdoch put nearly all his time and energy into making the *News* a profitable publication. He worked at lower levels of the paper to learn how it was produced. He also spent a lot of time in London at the successful *Daily Express*, learning how a successful newspaper was run.

In August 1953, just ten months after his father's death, Murdoch decided to fight his biggest

College Graduate

When Murdoch took over the Adelaide *News*, he had not yet graduated from college. He continued to take courses at Worcester College and to study for final exams in June 1953. Asa Briggs, a tutor, helped him study every day for nearly four months. Murdoch graduated with a third-class honors degree, nearly the lowest degree granted.

competitor. He began what he referred to as a lifelong series of battles with others and the world. The *Advertiser* had twice as many subscribers as the *News*, but that did not stop Murdoch.

The *News* published a weekly Sunday newspaper called the *Sunday Mail*. The *Advertiser* decided to print its own Sunday publication, giving Adelaide two Sunday papers. For nearly two years, the newspapers competed for the largest circulation. Murdoch enjoyed the challenge, and his *Sunday Mail* held up under the pressure.

In 1955, the rival companies agreed to merge their Sunday papers, publish the *Sunday Mail* together, and split the costs and the shares. Murdoch did not see it as a merger, however. He saw it as a chance to make the Sunday *Advertiser* disappear. Murdoch considered this a great victory.

During the 1950s, the *News* grew and flourished. Circulation increased, and profits grew. Then, Murdoch purchased the *Sunday Times*, a newspaper in Perth, located in Western Australia. He also bought small-town newspapers in Darwin, Alice Springs, and Mount Isa. He purchased *New Idea*, a women's magazine. His motto became "Expand or die."[1]

BECOMING A HUSBAND AND A FATHER

While busy expanding the family business, Murdoch also expanded his family. In 1956, the 25-year-old married Patricia Booker. She worked at a department store in Adelaide and had been a flight attendant. Marriage did not slow down Murdoch's business ventures. Even on his honeymoon, he checked on his newly acquired properties and kept a close eye on the *News*.

In the late 1950s, Murdoch's personal and professional lives continued to expand. Personally, he took on a new role as father when he and Patricia welcomed the birth of a daughter, Prudence. Professionally, he ventured into the world of television.

THE WORLD OF TELEVISION

Murdoch entered a different medium in 1958 when his company purchased Channel 9 in Adelaide. Television had been a mainstream household item in Australia for only two years, though television sets

Australian Television

Mainstream television arrived in Australia in 1956. Crowds gathered outside Sydney department store windows and in front of home television sets to watch the significant event. The first broadcast opened with Bruce Gyngell's words, "Welcome to television."[2] That year, Gyngell hosted the game show *Name That Tune*. Variety and game shows have played significant roles in Australian television.

had been a must-have in US homes since the mid-1940s. Murdoch went to the United States to learn about the television business. He visited television studios in Los Angeles, California, and New York City. He watched popular programs and decided which ones he could afford to buy for his station.

He also searched US culture for ideas to imitate in Australia. While he was in the United States, he bought copies of US newspapers and magazines to get ideas for his own publications. Then, he visited the offices of *TV Guide* in Philadelphia, Pennsylvania. He hoped to start a similar magazine in Australia.

When Murdoch returned to Adelaide, he immediately put his knowledge to work. Borrowing from the US publication, Murdoch launched an Australian version of *TV Guide* and set out to make television a winner. Channel 9 became a great success. The station was very profitable and gave Murdoch enough money to tackle his competitors in Sydney, the largest city in Australia.

PURCHASE IN SYDNEY

Three powerful families—the Fairfaxes, the Packers, and the Nortons—ran the newspaper industry in Sydney. In 1958, Ezra Norton retired. For two decades, his popular tabloid, the *Daily Mirror*, had competed fiercely against the *Evening Sun*, which was owned by the Fairfaxes.

Norton ended up selling the *Mirror* to the Fairfax family. The competition was now between the Fairfaxes and the Packers. But when the *Mirror* became a burden to the Fairfax business,

Sensational Stories

Murdoch's tabloids were often called yellow journalism. This type of publishing reports sensational stories, vulgar topics, and provocative photographs—often unfounded—that traditional newspapers would not generally print.

The term *yellow journalism* began in 1897. Newspapers in New York City were competing fiercely for sales. Joseph Pulitzer's *New York World* battled William Randolph Hearst's *New York Journal*. Both newspapers tried to increase circulation by sensationalizing some of their news. They featured crime stories and scandals sprinkled with shocking language and pictures. They embellished stories about the 1898 Spanish-American War. Some claimed the stories were packed with lies, but the public liked this kind of journalism, and circulation increased for both papers.

Murdoch exhibited this type of journalism in 1961, when a reporter sent to New Guinea to cover the clan wars there went into the jungle and failed to send copy back to Sydney on time. Murdoch's paper invented a story "including man-eating cannibals and shrunken heads" and published it in the paper under the missing reporter's name.[3] When the reporter came back from the jungle and read the article, he apparently sent Murdoch a telegram that said, "Nearest shrunken heads to Dutch New Guinea are in Sydney."[4]

Murdoch in 1960 with his new tabloid, the Daily Mirror

they looked for a new buyer—anyone but the Packers.
Murdoch stepped in. He purchased the *Mirror* for
what he called a bargain price. "I was amazed they
agreed," he said.[5] And reports spread that he danced
a jig after the agreement was signed.

Murdoch worked hard to make the *Mirror* into
the best-selling newspaper. Competition between
Murdoch and Frank Packer was fierce. Packer
declared a circulation war on the *Mirror* and vowed to

send Murdoch back to Adelaide. Murdoch purchased printing plants in three cities to be able to print more papers.

The *Mirror* published sensational stories that shocked and attracted a large audience. Murdoch's reporters would do almost anything to get a scandalous breaking story. The *Mirror* also ran contests offering expensive prizes such as cars, swimming pools, and houses. All of Murdoch's schemes and strategies paid off. The *Mirror* gained popularity, and circulation increased. Murdoch would celebrate a final victory over his rival by purchasing the *Daily Telegraph* from the aging Frank Packer in 1972.

MORE TELEVISION

Murdoch was always looking for another challenge and opportunity. In 1962, he purchased a struggling television station, Channel WIN 4, in Wollongong, New South Wales. Immediately, he visited Leonard Goldenson at ABC in New York City. There, Murdoch purchased exclusive Australian rights to everything ABC produced for the next five years.

Back in Australia, Frank Packer offered Murdoch a deal. If Murdoch would share his American television programs, Packer would give him one-fourth of the stock in his company and two seats on the board of directors. Murdoch did not hesitate to accept Packer's offer. He now owned and directed part of his archrival's company. Step by step, he was gaining control of Australia's media.

In ten years, Murdoch had acquired the Adelaide *News*, the Perth *Sunday Mail* and *Sunday Times*, and the Sydney *Mirror*. The newspapers covered the eastern, western, and southern portions of Australia. Murdoch also owned *New Idea* magazine and a weekly television guide. Two television stations and five-year rights to ABC's programs cemented Murdoch's position as one of Australia's top media magnates. But Australia would prove too small for Murdoch's far-reaching goals. He set his sights on the rest of the world.

By the late 1960s, Murdoch had become a busy businessman with interests in both newspaper publishing and television.

Murdoch's business holdings expanded to Hong Kong in the early 1960s.

EXPANDING THE EMPIRE

The 1960s brought more additions to Murdoch's media empire. In 1963, he went to Hong Kong and purchased 28 percent of Asia Magazines Ltd., a magazine publisher based in that city. The following year, he expanded his holdings to New Zealand, where he bought a major newspaper called the *Dominion*.

THE *AUSTRALIAN*

In 1964, Murdoch created a newspaper at home—the *Australian*. With a used printing press, he set up offices for a newspaper he hoped would one day be a national publication. He wanted it to reach people throughout Australia. Its home base was Canberra, a small town and the nation's capital.

Unlike Murdoch's sensational tabloids, the *Australian* was a serious newspaper. It competed against the *Times*, the only other newspaper in Canberra. At one time, Murdoch's father had wanted to buy the *Times*, but the owners, the Shakespeare family, would not sell it. Now Murdoch referred to the *Times* as "a tiny little very underdeveloped rag."[1] His goal was to put the paper out of business.

Almost immediately, the Shakespeares sold the *Times* to John Fairfax, Murdoch's chief competitor in Sydney. Within a month, Fairfax turned the newspaper into a professional-looking broadsheet. Also known as a broadside, this type of paper, which generally measures 15 inches (38 cm) by 24 inches (61 cm), is common in Britain. Murdoch took on the challenge and stepped up his efforts to publish a first-rate national newspaper of his own.

Murdoch and his editor, Max Newton, sold advertising space to businesses all over the continent and took out loans to finance their venture.

Murdoch put all his energy into creating a successful newspaper. Murdoch's staff caught the excitement of launching the *Australian*. In a few months, Murdoch and Newton were printing and distributing the publication throughout the nation.

Personal Life

While Murdoch was enjoying business success, his personal life was suffering. His wife, Pat, and daughter, Prudence, had stayed in Sydney while Murdoch launched the *Australian* in Canberra. Spending less time together was causing them to grow apart. "I was totally involved in the business," admitted Murdoch, and "probably very inconsiderate."[2] Instead of spending his spare time

Prudence Murdoch MacLeod

Murdoch's oldest child, Prudence, has not worked in the family business, but her husband has. In 1989, she married Scotsman Alasdair MacLeod. Prudence was opposed to her husband working for her father, but shortly after the couple married, Murdoch offered MacLeod a job despite Prudence's wishes. MacLeod accepted his offer and was made the managing director of Murdoch's company News Limited Community Newspapers.

The couple has three children: James, Angus, and Clementine. Prudence lives with her husband and children in Sydney.

Murdoch worked hard in London to establish himself on Fleet Street.

with his family, he went yachting with friends and fishing in the mountains. He frequented horse races, where he bet a great deal of his money.

Murdoch divorced his wife in the mid-1960s. He was given custody of Prudence, who was six years old at the time. He soon began dating 18-year-old Anna Torv, one of his employees at the *Daily Mirror*. Murdoch, Anna, and Prudence moved to London, where Murdoch and Anna were married in April 1967.

Although Murdoch lived in London, he still spent a lot of time in Australia. He had a second home about 20 miles (32 km) from Canberra. Murdoch and his wife hosted many parties there at their large stone house nestled on thousands of acres along the Murrumbridgee River.

The British Market

In 1968, Murdoch heard Britain's *News of the World* was possibly for sale. With a circulation of 6 million, it was one of Britain's most popular publications and considered "the granddaddy of Sunday tabloid journalism, accenting the underside of British life."[3] Its articles were scandalous and steamy. Murdoch resolved to purchase the tabloid, which had been owned by the Carr family for decades. His first move was to become the newspaper's managing director. In that position, he received 40 percent of the company's stock. Murdoch had entered the British publishing market. He was now part of Fleet Street, the London location of England's largest publishers as well as the nickname for the British press.

Murdoch wasted no time figuring out ways to purchase more stock in the company. He also completely transformed the newspaper's layout and staff. By 1969, Murdoch was elected chairman of the company and owned 49 percent of its shares—more than anyone else. He now controlled *News of the World*.

One of his first series of articles in the paper was about a scandal surrounding John Profumo, Britain's defense secretary. Six years earlier, Profumo had had an affair. It was one of the most highly publicized stories in British history. Profumo had since redeemed himself with a life of charitable work, but Murdoch dredged up the old scandal to sell newspapers. Sales of *News of the World* went up, and Murdoch was pleased. Murdoch discussed the issue in an interview:

Fleet Street

From the 1500s until the 1980s, Fleet Street in London was home to most of the British press. Wynkyn de Worde established the first print shop there. He was an apprentice to William Caxton, a British merchant and printer. Richard Pynson set up his publishing house and print shop there at about the same time. Other printers followed.

In 1702, London's first daily newspaper—the *Daily Courant*—set up its presses on Fleet Street, above the White Hart Inn. It was a one-page newspaper with two columns. The newspaper merged with the *Daily Gazetteer* in 1735.

Today, most British newspapers are no longer located on Fleet Street. Reuters, a British news agency, was the last to leave in 2005. The street is now filled with inns, law offices, and investment banks such as Goldman Sachs.

The term Fleet Street means more than a London street. It speaks of an era when newspapers still rolled off the presses and were hauled by train to every part of England and Ireland. In journalism, Fleet Street still refers to the British press.

I don't agree it's sleazy for a minute. Nor do I agree that it's unfair to the man. I have the greatest sympathy with him, but it doesn't alter the fact that everybody knows what happened. Certainly it's going to sell newspapers.[4]

THE FROST INTERVIEW

Murdoch quickly became the talk of London. David Frost, one of Britain's most well-known journalists, wanted an interview with this new controversial journalist. Frost had just launched his newest television program, *The David Frost Show*, and he wanted to have Murdoch as a guest. The interview would be remembered as one of Frost's most remarkable programs.

In the interview, Frost attacked Murdoch fiercely for his shocking series of stories about Profumo. Murdoch argued that the story had already been published in several books. Frost told Murdoch it was not the British way of doing things— Murdoch's focus on past indecencies did not seem proper to the British. Frost pushed Murdoch to explain

News of the World

As of 2010, Murdoch still owned *News of the World*, the popular British tabloid. The paper has been repeatedly sued for libel and charged with grossly irresponsible journalism. Brad Pitt and Angelina Jolie filed a lawsuit against it in 2010 for false claims about their relationship.

what good came out of printing the story in his newspaper. Murdoch answered calmly that there is nothing wrong with "telling a story twice."[5]

Murdoch left the interview irate. On his way out, he said to the producer of the show, "I will buy this company."[6] And one day he would.

The interview made both men famous. Frost had made Murdoch into a villain—confirming what many British viewers already believed about the Australian—and they enjoyed condemning him. Murdoch, on the other hand, had the fuel he needed to seek revenge on Frost and the traditional British establishment.

The David Frost Show

The David Frost Show aired from 1969 to 1972. Following Frost's 1969 interview with Murdoch, the angry businessman threatened to buy the company. And he followed through on his threat. Murdoch bought controlling interest in London Weekend Television between 1969 and 1970. The company produced the show. He fired board members and changed the programming. Nearly 40 years after the interview, Murdoch revealed to journalist and biographer Michael Wolff about Frost, "I feel like saying, 'I'll get [him] one day,' but he'll die before I get him."[7]

The *Sun*

One way for Murdoch to get revenge on his British critics was to buy more British newspapers. In 1969, the *Sun* went up for sale, and Murdoch purchased it. The *Sun* was an immediate success. Murdoch credited the paper's initial popularity to an aggressive television advertising campaign.

The *Sun* was also successful because it focused on the young working class. Its audience was quite different from other British newspapers, which targeted an older population whom Murdoch considered snobbish. The *Sun* published articles about pop culture, giving space to news about television, radio, and sports. Like Adelaide's *Mirror*, the *Sun* offered contests with prizes. The paper also included articles and pictures on sexual topics and news about divorces. Both issues shocked readers and critics. Many said the newspaper had no principles.

The *Sun* regularly criticized and made fun of the British royal family. Prince Philip, Queen Elizabeth II's husband, did not appreciate Murdoch and his articles about Britain's royalty. Prince Philip would be in conflict with Murdoch for decades to come.

The *Sun* also took a bold political stance. It condemned capital punishment, South Africa's racist system of apartheid, racism, and the Vietnam War—all hot topics. Murdoch's views brought him attention and power. However, established liberal Britons viewed the publisher as dangerous. But the more criticism Murdoch received, the harder he worked to succeed.

The Kidnapping

Some despised Murdoch and his
publications so much that they tried
to shut him down. Others just wanted
to harm him and take his money. At
the end of 1969, Rupert and Anna
were in Australia for Christmas.
They had lent their Rolls-Royce
to Alick McKay, one of Murdoch's
top executives in Great Britain. On
December 29, McKay's wife, Muriel,
took the borrowed car to go shopping. She did not
return. She had been kidnapped. When kidnappers
demanded a ransom, it became obvious that Muriel
McKay had been mistaken for Anna Murdoch.

The kidnappers realized their mistake and made a
ransom call to Alick McKay. The male caller said,

> We are Mafia M3. We tried to get Rupert Murdoch's wife.
> We couldn't get her so we took yours instead. You have a
> million by Wednesday night or we will kill her.[8]

The kidnappers were eventually caught, arrested,
tried, and imprisoned. Muriel McKay was never
found, and only the kidnappers know what happened
to her.

Anna's Books

Anna Murdoch is an
author. Three of her novels have been published.
In Her Own Image (1986)
is about the courage
women need in a world
of men. *Family Business*
(1988) is a tale about a
newspaper dynasty. *Coming to Terms* (1993) is
about a woman who travels to New York to care for
her invalid uncle.

Although Murdoch had been doing business internationally for years, the kidnapping made him famous worldwide. It also gave his enemies a weapon to use against him and his media empire. One cynical letter used the incident to attack Murdoch's two British newspapers. It read,

> *I will let Mrs. McKay go if the* News of the World *and the* Sun *publicly announce that they will not corrupt our kids any more by printing all that filth.* [9]

Richard Ingrams, editor of a small paper called the *Private Eye*, constantly attacked Murdoch—"the Dirty Digger," as he came to be called. He accused Murdoch of vandalizing the British press.

Murdoch argued that he was only giving the public what it wanted. But he would not live amidst the British criticism much longer. In the early 1970s, he and his family left Great Britain and moved to the United States. There, he would continue expanding his empire and meet new critics. ⌣

In the late 1960s, Murdoch was growing his business and his family, which included his second wife, Anna, and daughter Elisabeth.

Chapter

5

Murdoch's desire to expand his company led him to San Antonio, Texas, where he bought his first US newspapers.

BUSINESS IN THE UNITED STATES

In the early 1970s, Murdoch's British and Australian business ventures were thriving. The United States was on the horizon as a possibility for expansion. In 1973, Murdoch moved his family across the Atlantic to San Antonio, Texas. For years, he had wanted to extend his company to the United States. He chose San Antonio because newspapers were for sale there. His first purchases were the *Express*, the *News*, and a Sunday paper produced jointly by both newspapers.

As had been the case previously, Murdoch entered the US newspaper industry as an underdog. He competed with the *Light*, a successful newspaper owned by the powerful Hearst Corporation. Murdoch liked a challenge, and he was happy to have a foothold in the United States.

Murdoch set out to improve his newspapers and defeat Hearst. He spiced up his papers' articles, made them more readable, offered huge prizes for contests, and advertised on television. Within a decade, the papers would be more popular than the *Light*.

The *National Star*

Murdoch was not satisfied with only local newspapers in San Antonio. He wanted a national publication. In 1974, he founded the *National Star*, a sensational supermarket tabloid modeled after the popular *National Enquirer*, which had been around since 1926. The *National Star* focused on celebrity gossip, crime stories, and sensational news.

For the first few months, Murdoch did most of the work at the publication—editing, writing, and layout. The tabloid targeted women readers. In 1976, the paper's new subtitle became "The American Women's Weekly." The word *National* was dropped from the title, and the tabloid became the *Star*. In fewer than ten years, the *Star* would make $12 million per year and have a circulation of 4 million. It nearly caught up with the *National Enquirer*.

The *New York Post*

Meanwhile, Murdoch went to New York City to look for more newspapers to buy. He wanted to own a newspaper in the largest US city. About that time, Dorothy Schiff, a prominent, liberal New York socialite, was ready to retire. She decided to sell the *New York Post*, which she had owned since 1939. Murdoch purchased the *New York Post* in 1976 for $30 million. He was happy about this major acquisition. The *Post* was the United States' thirteenth-oldest newspaper, founded in 1801 by Alexander Hamilton. It was the nation's longest-running daily news publication.

Tabloid Headlines

Murdoch launched his San Antonio newspapers with sensational and sometimes unforgettable headlines. The most memorable headlines included "Armies of Insects Marching on SA," "Handless Body Found," "Army to Poison 350 Puppies," and "Killer Bees Move North."

Murdoch believed US journalism was stuffy. Over the next year, he changed the *Post* into a tabloid. The shocking headlines, gossip columns, sex scandals, and crime stories were outrageous, but popular. Readers particularly liked the sports section. Some also enjoyed the outspoken editorials that promoted conservative political views.

Still, the *Post* received criticism from its onset for its sensationalism and conservatism. Some dubbed the publication "a screaming tabloid" that only promoted Murdoch's views.[1] Nevertheless, circulation nearly doubled over the next decade.

Serial Killer Helps the *New York Post*

Circulation of Murdoch's *New York Post* soared in 1977 with coverage of the Son of Sam murders. Son of Sam, a serial killer named David Berkowitz, terrorized New York City from July 1976 through August 1977, when he was arrested. He killed young couples parked in secluded areas away from busy city life.

The media covered the serial murders with great detail and speculated on the identity of the killer. The *New York Post* competed with the *Daily News* for the most thrilling coverage. On May 30, 1977, Jimmy Breslin, columnist for the *Daily News*, received a handwritten letter signed by Son of Sam. Breslin printed portions of the letter in the newspaper and asked the killer to turn himself in. That day, more than 1 million copies of the *Daily News* were sold. The article sent panic through New York and gripped the city in fear.

The *New York Post* would not be outdone. It retaliated and printed letters Berkowitz had written to an old girlfriend. Both newspapers were criticized for their extreme style of journalism. In the end, the *New York Post* had the most sensational coverage. Sales rose dramatically, and the tabloid went from near bankruptcy to making huge profits.

Murdoch's New York publications were not limited to the *Post*. The publisher continued to look for business opportunities in the US metropolis. In 1977, he acquired *New York* magazine, *New West* magazine, and the *Village Voice* newspaper. Some people claimed Murdoch was on a New York buying spree.

Newspaper Strike

In 1978, New York's newspaper unions went on strike. The people who ran the presses walked off the job. Three major newspapers—the *New York Times*, the *Daily News*, and the *New York Post*—shut down.

For a while, the owners of the three newspapers worked together to end the strike. But finally, Murdoch went on his own. He made a personal deal with the unions. If the workers would return to their jobs at the *New York Post*, Murdoch would go along with any deal the unions ended up making with the *New York Times* and the *Daily News*. Murdoch's *New York Post* was soon back on the streets, while the other newspapers were still negotiating with the unions. It was another month before an agreement was reached and the other newspapers were once again distributed on the streets.

Murdoch, center, walks from the New York Post *in 1978 as pickets continued walking in the third week of the city's newspaper strike.*

Murdoch's competitors were not happy with his union deal. By the end of the 1970s, Murdoch was unpopular with some in the New York City publishing industry. Josef Barletta, general manager of the *Daily News*, wrote,

> *In Murdoch's world there are no rules. . . . Now that he has shown how he works, we'll do it too. We're willing to play the game with him by his rules if that's what he wants.* [2]

The executive editor of the *New York Times* called Murdoch "a bad element, practicing mean, ugly, violent journalism." [3]

GROWING FAMILY

The Gambler

For decades, news stories about Murdoch have drawn attention to his gambling. Headlines have read, "Rupert Murdoch— The Gambler's Rolling High," "Murdoch, the Gambler Who Can't Bear to Lose," and "Murdoch, the Gambler Who Always Wins." In the 1970s, Murdoch's newspapers offered simple forms of gambling, such as sports pools, lotto, and bingo.

Murdoch's business was growing, and so was his family. He now had four children—Prudence from his first marriage and three from his second. Elisabeth had been born in 1968, Lachlan in 1971, and James in 1972. The family lived in New York City, but wife Anna preferred Australia and pressured her husband to move back. She wanted her children raised there.

Murdoch also preferred Australia for his children. He planned to return with them and set up permanent headquarters there for his business. When asked whether his decision to settle in Australia was for personal or business reasons, he responded,

> *Purely personal. I think it is a lottery whatever happens to your children, but quite a compelling reason is not to have my children educated in the public-school system in England because I feel they could never get the old school tie off their necks. If they [my children] want to lead a life in newspapers, if they choose that, they will grow up with better values in Australia than anywhere else I can think of.[4]*

Rupert and Anna Murdoch with their three children, photographed in 1977

Since Murdoch's business ventures in the United States were solid, he turned his attention back to his native land. He changed his Australian business name from News Limited to News Corporation Ltd. And he changed his focus to Australian television.

In 1979, Murdoch set his business sights on Australia's Channel 10, Sydney's third-largest television station. It was not for sale, but Murdoch bought enough shares in the parent company, United Telecasters Ltd., to give him control of it.

That same year, Murdoch went after Channel 10 in Melbourne. The two stations broadcast to the country's two largest cities. Together, they held 60 percent of Australia's advertising profits. Again, the station was not for sale, so Murdoch purchased shares in the parent company, Ansett Transport Industries.

Ansett owned the television station. It was also Australia's second-largest airline company. Ansett was having financial problems, so the price of shares was low. Murdoch took advantage of the bargain price and bought enough shares to become Ansett's largest shareholder. He now had control of Channel 10 in Melbourne as well as control of a major Australian airline company.

Murdoch's acquisitions during the 1970s were bringing him greater wealth and power. His company was becoming a huge media conglomerate. His growing domination of newspapers and television was giving him international political power. In the next decade, Murdoch would influence politics worldwide, including in Australia, Great Britain, and the United States.

As Murdoch's media empire has grown, so too has his
political influence.

Murdoch circa 1980

POLITICAL CONNECTIONS

Murdoch's purchase of Ansett thrust him into a new industry—the competitive world of commercial air travel. In 1980, when Ansett needed to buy new airplanes, Murdoch visited Boeing's headquarters in Seattle, Washington.

At the time, Jimmy Carter was in his third year as president of the United States. The US economy was in a deep recession, and companies were eager to sell their products. As the cost of living increased, unemployment did the same. Americans were not happy. Carter was on the Democratic primary ticket to run for a second term. He was running against well-known Democrats such as Massachusetts senator Edward Kennedy and California governor Jerry Brown. The *New York Post* endorsed Carter in the primary.

Six days after the endorsement, Murdoch was approved for a $209 million loan that would allow him to purchase 21 new commercial Boeing jets. The huge loan had an unusually low interest rate. Coincidentally, Murdoch had eaten lunch that day with President Carter at the White House. Suspicions developed that Murdoch and Carter had made a deal—approval for

Supporting Margaret Thatcher

Murdoch liked Margaret Thatcher, prime minister of the United Kingdom from 1979 to 1990. Like President Reagan, she was a conservative whose political ideas fit well with Murdoch's. In general, his newspapers and other publications supported Thatcher.

Murdoch never came right out and told his editors to write in favor of Thatcher. However, he would send them pro-Thatcher articles he said were worth reading. He criticized headlines that seemed hard on Thatcher and told his editors to have more conviction. He insisted on conviction. His editors took that to mean pro-Thatcher viewpoints.

a massive low-interest loan in exchange for political endorsement by Murdoch's newspaper.

FULL SENATE INVESTIGATION

Wisconsin senator William Proxmire chaired the Senate Committee on Banking, Housing, and Urban Affairs. He called for a full investigation of Murdoch and the loan he had received. Proxmire and other senators thought Carter may have given Murdoch a special deal in return for political support.

On May 12 and 13, 1980, Murdoch testified before the US Senate. Murdoch stated, "My luncheon with the President was totally unconnected to the Ansett purchase of Boeing aircraft and accompanying . . . loan."[1] Senator Proxmire reminded Murdoch of the huge influence the media has on public opinion. Proxmire asked Murdoch whether he had a code of ethics to avoid any conflicts of interest, a situation in which his personal interests might influence his business decisions. "Of course we do, sir," said Murdoch. "There is no conflict of interest here unless it's in the eye of the beholder."[2]

Murdoch was found not guilty of any unlawful activities. All charges against him were dropped. Proxmire ended the hearings by scolding the bank

Murdoch's purchase of several new airplanes was made possible through a loan by a US bank that drew the attention—and disapproval—of many.

that gave Murdoch the low-interest loan, adding that he was still troubled by what he saw as an incredible series of coincidences. But then Proxmire complimented Murdoch:

> Well, I want to say that you are a remarkable man, Mr. Murdoch. We have had a lot of witnesses before this committee, but I was especially impressed with what a quick study you are. You seem to know a whale of a lot about an industry you've just gotten into. You are very refreshing, intelligent and an effective witness, and responsive.[3]

Murdoch went on to make Ansett a profitable company. By the end of the 1980s, the airline was servicing 60 Australian ports with 6.5 million customers.

SUPPORT FOR RONALD REAGAN

In 1980, President Carter won the Democratic primary. In November, Carter was up against Republican nominee Ronald Reagan. While the *New York Post* had endorsed Carter in the primary, the paper supported Reagan for the November election.

Reagan won the election by a landslide. Republicans gained majority control of the Senate for the first time in 25 years. Murdoch continued to back Reagan during his two terms in office. Murdoch enjoyed Reagan's conservative politics, which would prevail during the 1980s.

Support for Reagan

Murdoch supported Ronald Reagan in his 1980 presidential race against incumbent Jimmy Carter. The *New York Post* regularly published articles backing Reagan.

MORE BRITISH NEWSPAPERS

Murdoch's political influence in the 1980s was due largely to his purchase of two more British

Murdoch has not hesitated in supporting politicians publicly, including Ronald Reagan.

newspapers. In 1981, he acquired the London *Times* and the *Sunday Times*. They were the newspapers once owned by his father's mentor, Lord Northcliffe.

The *Times* and *Sunday Times* were two of Britain's most prominent publications. Roy Thomson, a Canadian, had owned the papers since 1959. But when Thomson died in 1976, the newspapers barely survived. Thomson's son, Ken, did not want the business. In October 1981, the newspapers went up for sale. Powerful owners of other newspapers were interested in purchasing the two publications. Murdoch was also interested and put in a bid just before the December 31 deadline.

The unions and the *Times* board of directors both favored Murdoch. They remembered how he had made the *Sun* successful and created new jobs. The *Times* had been struggling for years, and they believed Murdoch could turn it around. Murdoch was chosen as the buyer for the *Times* and the *Sunday Times*. After purchasing the papers, Murdoch kept Harold Evans on staff. Evans had been the editor of the *Sunday Times* since 1959. Murdoch put him in charge of the *Times*, a daily publication.

The demands of a daily newspaper were stressful for Evans and other journalists. The *Times* was having financial problems, and there was conflict among staff members. In March 1982, Murdoch asked for Evans's resignation, which he gave reluctantly. Less than two years later, Evans published *Good Times, Bad Times*, a book in which he criticized Murdoch

Updating the *Times*

The *Times* is a British newspaper that dates back to 1785, when it was called the *Daily Universal Register*. When Murdoch bought the *Times* in 1981, he phased out old printing methods and introduced computerized printing. The introduction of newer printing technology reduced the number of employees by 20 percent.

and characterized him as the personification of evil. Murdoch ignored the book and told an interviewer, "Harry wanted to be loved by everybody. But he ended up being loved by nobody."[4]

MORE US MEDIA

In the United States, the *New York Post* was also struggling. It carried only 6 percent of the advertising for all New York City newspapers. The *New York Times* had 56 percent, and the *Daily News* had 38 percent. Murdoch finally concluded that New York did not have enough of the working-class readers

Problems in New York

When Murdoch moved to New York City, he and his family were shunned for a time. Murdoch attempted to enroll his children in an elite private school, but they were denied admission.

In 1977, Murdoch also had trouble with Clay Felker, his good friend and one of the founders of *New York* magazine. Murdoch wanted to purchase the magazine. Felker did not like the idea. Writers for *New York* did not want Murdoch to buy the magazine. They did not want Murdoch as their boss.

Murdoch bought the magazine in a hostile takeover. Felker, who served as the magazine's editor, threatened to resign. Murdoch wanted him to stay on, and Felker said he would take the advice of his staff. The journalists for the magazine held protest meetings, vowed never to work for Murdoch, and ridiculed him for being foreign and for publishing subpar material. The writers publicly expressed their dissatisfaction with Murdoch—and their determination to resist him.

There was a court hearing in which the judge ruled that Murdoch's purchase of the magazine would stand. Felker resigned, as did several writers and staff members.

Irresistible

Murdoch has wanted to purchase the *New York Times* for decades. Biographer Michael Wolff wrote, "It's obviously irresistible to him. I've watched him go through the numbers, plot out a merger, . . . and fantasize about the staff's quitting en masse as soon as he entered the sacred temple."[6]

who appreciated the *New York Post*'s sensational tabloid style. Murdoch tried to purchase the *Daily News*, but the owner, the Tribune Company, refused. A *Daily News* headline announced, "Trib to Rupert: Drop Dead."[5]

Murdoch searched for other US newspapers to purchase. He found one in Massachusetts—the *Boston Herald*. It was published in direct competition with the *Boston Globe*. He purchased the *Herald* in 1982. Although the *Herald* remained in second place in Boston, its circulation increased by more than 100,000 the first year.

In the mid-1980s, Murdoch turned his attention to entertainment—US film and television. He set his sights on 20th Century Fox film studios and a group of top-notch US television stations. His entry into US television would not be easy, but, as always, Murdoch would accomplish what he set out to do. ⌐

As the 1970s drew to a close, Murdoch continued to grow his collection of newspapers, reflecting his love of the newspaper industry.

The success of Murdoch's company, News Corp., is undeniable.

US FILM AND
TELEVISION

Many of Murdoch's ventures proved successful over the years, but some did not perform well. In the early 1980s, the *Post* was failing, but popular newspapers such as London's *Sun* kept Murdoch's business strong.

Murdoch started looking at other business opportunities. He spent less time in Australia, which is where Anna lived, and more time in the United States. He believed he could best fulfill his goals there, where there was more focus on the entertainment industry.

Worldwide Media Holdings

Murdoch's media holdings are broad and varied. He operates businesses on six continents that control a variety of media, including newspapers, magazines, television, cable, satellite, film, and Internet.

IN THE MEDIA

By the mid-1980s, Murdoch was well known in the United States. As he purchased more US media outlets, his influence on—and control over—what Americans could read and view increased. As his power and wealth increased, Murdoch attracted more media attention. In early 1984, the successful businessman was the subject of articles in two magazines that focus on finances and business.

In January, *Forbes* magazine featured the media mogul in its cover story, "What Does This Man Want?" In his article, journalist Thomas J. O'Hanlon described Murdoch as "part accountant, part gambler, part brilliant marketer, part shrewd journalist."[1]

Fortune magazine published an article about Murdoch the following month. In "Rupert Murdoch's Motley Empire," Richard I. Kirkland and Gwen Kinkead wrote less favorably about the publishing tycoon: "Murdoch's tabloids luridly depict a world in which fiendish criminals prey on women and children, evil immigrants menace the natives, and most government affairs are too tedious to note."[2]

"Murdoch is someone who seems to have been allowed to grow unchecked, like . . . some sort of monster in a science fiction movie, *The Blob* or something. And you keep waiting for somebody to sort of shape him up and push him back in, but it doesn't happen."[3]

—*Tom Shales, TV critic,* Washington Post

Murdoch's coverage by the media continued that spring. This time, television took an interest. Murdoch was featured on ABC's *20/20* prime-time television program. The segment gave viewers an idea of Murdoch's personal life as camera crews filmed him inside his London apartment and at his posh New York City triplex on Fifth Avenue. They filmed him leisurely taking a walk in Central Park with his wife, Anna, and their children, Elisabeth, Lachlan, and James, ages 16, 13, and 11, respectively.

But the biographical piece was interested in Murdoch the businessman as well. Barbara Walters,

the show's cohost, conducted the interview.
Walters addressed Murdoch's style of newspaper
publishing, accusing him of appealing to people's
lowest instincts. Not one to back down, Murdoch
responded to the 20/20 host:

> *Well, there's nothing wrong with talking to the masses. You*
> *know, William Shakespeare wrote for the masses. I think if he*
> *was writing today, he'd probably be the chief scriptwriter on*
> All in the Family *or* Dallas *[popular television shows in*
> *the 1970s and 1980s].* [4]

MOVIES AND TELEVISION

While increasing numbers of Americans were
taking notice of Murdoch, he was continuing to eye
new business ventures in his adopted land. Murdoch
was paying close attention to Hollywood. Film
studio 20th Century Fox was struggling financially
following a string of unsuccessful movies. In
March 1984, Murdoch purchased 50 percent of the
company from owner Marvin Davis.

In 1985, Murdoch and Davis tried to buy seven
television stations from Metromedia, a company
owned by John Kluge. The stations were located in
major US cities: New York City, Boston, Los Angeles,

Chicago, Dallas, Houston, and Washington DC. An article in the May 6, 1985, edition of the *New York Times* read, "Rupert's a man who's always thrilled with a new challenge. . . . He's always ready to climb Mount Everest. He has a broad attention span. Very broad."[5]

But Murdoch could not purchase the stations. A US law stated only US citizens could own more than 20 percent of any US television station. Murdoch would not be stopped. He applied to become a US citizen.

Citizenship was not the only issue.

Newspaper Workers on Strike

In January 1986, 6,000 members of the British newspaper unions went on strike. The strike followed several years of negotiations between News International and the workers' unions. News International was part of News Corporation, which publishes four British Papers: the *Times*, the *Sunday Times*, the *Sun*, and *News of the World*. Murdoch's newspaper presses on London's Fleet Street were in danger of being shut down. Murdoch fired all 6,000 employees and replaced the entire workforce. He immediately moved from Fleet Street and relocated to a London district known as Wapping.

The fired employees demonstrated outside the Wapping plant and organized marches. In addition to numerous print workers and supporters, local residents also joined the demonstrations.

Police made sure the demonstrators did not interfere with Murdoch's business. Murdoch's workers were bused to the plant to ensure their safety. Protestors tried to prevent the newspapers from getting to the trains for distribution, but Murdoch transported the newspapers by truck. Violence ensued several times.

Murdoch's plant at Wapping had the support of the British government. In the end, the boycott proved unsuccessful. During the strike, which lasted more than a year, Murdoch's papers were printed and delivered daily.

Murdoch's fame and fortune have connected him with the world's rich and famous, including actress Elizabeth Taylor at a party in the 1980s.

A Federal Communications Commission (FCC) regulation prohibited one individual from owning a newspaper and a television station in the same city. Since one of the Metromedia television stations was in New York City, Murdoch would have to give up ownership of the *New York Post*. The idea of giving up even one of his newspapers was difficult.

Becoming a US Citizen

Murdoch would not give up his goal of owning US television stations, and on September 4, 1985, he officially became a US citizen. And while some questioned Murdoch's loyalty and motives, others were delighted with his new status as an American.

Mark Fowler was chairman of the FCC. He welcomed Murdoch's entry into US television. Fowler wanted the FCC to lift its prohibition of a person owning a newspaper and a television station in the same city. Fowler and the FCC would soon approve Murdoch's purchase of considerably more media, including business that Murdoch would merge into a single entity: Fox.

Murdoch leaves the US District Court in Manhattan with his citizenship papers after becoming a US citizen in September 1985.

The 20th Century Fox logo

THE BIRTH OF FOX

In October 1985, Murdoch announced his plan to create a fourth US television network. The Fox Broadcasting Company would compete with ABC, CBS, and NBC. Soon after, he paid $325 million to buy out Marvin Davis's

half ownership in 20th Century
Fox films. In March 1986, the FCC
approved Murdoch's purchase of the
six Metromedia television stations.
Murdoch was now the sole owner of a
US film studio and six US television
stations that broadcast to 22 percent
of US households. He combined
them into a new company: Fox Inc. It
would be known simply as Fox.

Murdoch's Fox television network
debuted its first program in 1986 on
October 9. *The Late Show* was hosted by
comedienne Joan Rivers. It got off to a strong start
but quickly fell in the ratings. Rivers quit the show in
1987, and a series of guest hosts filled in. The lack of
success of this first program did not stop Murdoch
from adding new series. More programs quickly
followed on the heels of *The Late Show*.

PRIME-TIME TELEVISION

On April 5, 1987, Fox aired its first prime-time
shows—*Married . . . with Children* and *The Tracey Ullman
Show*. That night, the two 30-minute programs ran
back-to-back at 7:00, 8:00, and 9:00. Every week,

Fox's The Simpsons *is a staple in US pop culture.*

wearing Bart T-shirts. They picked up on unique words and phrases Bart used—called Bartisms—and made them part of their vocabulary. *The Simpsons* proved that an animated television show could be a prime-time hit. Fox added more of them, including *King of the Hill* and *Family Guy,* in the late 1990s.

Mainstream Success

Fox was not yet a threat to ABC, CBS, or NBC, but its popularity was growing rapidly. In 1993,

Fox took exclusive coverage of National Football League (NFL) games away from CBS. Well-known football players-turned-sportscasters, such as Pat Summerall, John Madden, and Terry Bradshaw, went over to Fox. That year, Fox increased its programming to seven nights a week.

In the mid-1990s, Fox launched several soap operas for younger audiences. Popular shows such as *Beverly Hills 90210* and *Melrose Place* helped Fox on its climb to the top. The debut of *The X-Files* in 1993 marked the beginning of a series success, both in current airplay and syndication. In 1995, Fox launched *MADtv*.

Murdoch's film studio, 20th Century Fox, was also celebrating a huge success. The movie *Home Alone*, released on November 16, 1990, was a box office hit. Moviegoers liked the misadventures of the boy named Kevin, whose parents accidentally left him at home while they rushed off to vacation in Europe.

Fox's Most Successful Show

The Fox hit *The Simpsons* first appeared on the network in 1987 as short animated skits for *The Tracey Ullman Show*. In December 1989, it became its own half-hour prime-time show. Its premiere episode was the Christmas special "Simpsons Roasting on an Open Fire." In September 2009, *The Simpsons* began its twenty-first season on Fox. The popular show has won numerous awards. At the end of the twentieth century, *Time* magazine named it the century's best television series. The show has had such a strong presence in US pop culture that some of its slang terms have been accepted into leading English dictionaries, including Homer Simpson's "d'oh."

The movie became the second-highest-grossing film of the year. Other blockbusters in the 1990s included episodes one, two, and three of the *Star Wars* saga and *Titanic*.

EXPANDING TO CABLE

Fox expanded to cable channels during the 1990s. In 1994, it started FX, a cable network that featured reruns of shows no longer airing new episodes. It also aired a hodgepodge of travel shows and stories told by roving reporters. The Fox Movie Channel began in 1994, featuring commercial-free, uncut movies. Most of the movies were produced by 20th Century Fox.

In October 1996, Murdoch launched the Fox News Channel. Murdoch had more than money in mind when he launched Fox News. All news organizations have a perspective, and Murdoch's new channel would offer a distinct perspective different from other sources. Fox presents a politically

Buying the *Post*—Again

In 1993, Murdoch bought back the *New York Post*, the newspaper he had been forced to sell in 1988. An FCC regulation had barred him from owning a newspaper and a television station in the same city. However, a number of politicians persuaded the FCC to make an exception for Murdoch. Five years later, he was back as the owner of the conservative daily paper.

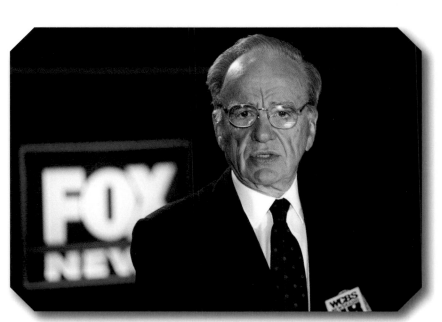

Murdoch launched his now-popular Fox News Channel in 1996.

conservative view. He created the channel to offer viewers an alternative to news offered by CNN, MSNBC, and other national news outlets. Murdoch explained, "They reflect the almost monolithic attitude of the press coming out of the *New York Times,* the *Boston Globe,* the *Washington Post*, and the three networks follow it exactly."[2]

The channel's well-known slogan is "Fair and Balanced." Fox is also advertised as "The Most Powerful Name in News." Fast-paced news coverage during the day was interspersed with interviews

and opinion shows such as *The O'Reilly Report* (now
The O'Reilly Factor) and *Hannity & Colmes* (now *Hannity*).
Fox News Alerts interrupted the programming with
breaking news. Fox News maintained that its hard
news on weekdays was objective. It called the rest of
its programming editorial or opinion journalism.

In 1996, Murdoch's company purchased several
cable sports channels and renamed them Fox Sports
Net (FSN). FSN featured play-by-play broadcasts
of major sporting events. It also aired pregame,
postgame, and weekly shows that focused on a
particular team.

In the late 1990s, Fox News experienced a huge
growth in ratings. By 2001, it was the top-rated cable
news network, a position it continued to hold in 2010.
In 2009, the network's popular news program *The
O'Reilly Factor* marked its tenth consecutive year as
television's top-rated cable news program.

The Fox network experienced the same success.
By the end of the 1990s, Fox was an established
fourth network, after ABC, NBC, and CBS.
Audiences were growing for both the network and
the cable channels. But in the twenty-first century,
Fox's ratings soared.

Bill O'Reilly hosts his talk show, titled The O'Reilly Factor, *for the Fox News Channel.*

In 2001, Murdoch wed for the third time.

THE TWENTY-FIRST CENTURY

or Murdoch, the twentieth century ended in financial success, and he entered the twenty-first century doing well, at least professionally. News Corp. was making a healthy profit, and his Fox television stations were soaring in the ratings.

But Murdoch's personal life was not doing as well. In June 1999, Rupert and Anna went through a bitter divorce, ending their 32-year marriage. Anna received a settlement valued at $200 million.

Seventeen days after the divorce, the 68-year-old Murdoch married 30-year-old Wendi Deng. She had recently been hired as vice president of Star TV, Murdoch's Asian satellite television network, when Murdoch met the young executive. In 2001, the couple had their first child, Grace. Their second daughter, Chloe, was born in 2003.

Fox Television Soars

Opportunities and success continued for Murdoch. Fox Broadcasting was now focusing on reality television with programs such as *Joe Millionaire*. The last episode of its first season attracted more than 40 million viewers. Other Fox reality series included *World's Wildest Police Videos* and *When Animals Attack!*

Fox also added more cable channels—Fox College Sports, Fuel TV, Fox Reality Channel, and Fox Business Network. And new dramas were launched, including *24*, *The O.C.*, *House*, and *Bones*. New comedies included *The Bernie Mac Show* and *Malcolm in the Middle*. But Fox's greatest achievement was *American Idol*.

American Idol launched in 2002. By the end of 2009, it was one of the most popular shows on television. Largely because of *American Idol*, Fox had become the highest-rated television network for people ages 18 to 49. In 2008, Fox surpassed CBS and became the nation's most popular network for all ages.

CHARGING FOR NEWS

As computers became a common household item in the 1990s, printed newspapers suffered. Internet users could access their news online, and newspaper advertising and circulation dwindled. Some predicted that newspapers would become a thing of the past. And, while circulation of print newspapers has declined, readership of online news has increased.

"By the time Rupert Murdoch retires to his Australian farm in the twenty-first century, his current vulgar image will have faded, and he will be regarded as a sage who followed opportunity where it led and put together a global empire in what may be the twenty-first century's greatest industry, communications."[1]
—Thomas J. O'Hanlon, "What Does this Man Want?"

The year 2008 was financially tough for News Corp. Profits declined, largely due to a huge reduction in newspaper subscriptions. In May 2009, News Corp. announced that all of its newspapers would charge for access to their content. By that time, Murdoch's

Wall Street Journal had been charging for online subscriptions for a couple of years.

One thing was clear: Murdoch was going to take advantage of the newer medium of the Internet to make money. In July 2010, two of Murdoch's British papers, the *Times* and the *Sunday Times*, began charging users to access content online. And by mid-September, plans were announced for Britain's top Sunday paper, *News of the World*, to charge as well. *News of the World* is a tabloid, and analyst Douglas McCabe noted how the difference in newspapers may be reflected in a difference in online subscribers:

> *In demographic terms you'd expect the audience to be slightly less likely to pay for online content than* Times *readers. And in terms of unique content, while the* News of the World *does break stories, in an online world, news tends to remain exclusive for a short period of time.*[2]

Data had not yet revealed to the public how successful these papers' sites have performed since charging for access. Depending on the paper's success with this online venture, it seemed likely that Murdoch would remain true to his word and other online papers would follow, making Murdoch a leader in yet another facet of media.

Continuing to Expand His Empire

The new century brought new additions as Murdoch continued what some have called a lifelong spending spree. In 2003, he paid $6 billion to buy DirecTV, a US satellite television company. Two years later, he bought Intermix Media Inc., which owned MySpace and other social networking Web sites. The deal cost him $580 million and made him a major player in the online realm. That same year, Murdoch spent $650 million to acquire Imagine Games Network (IGN), an online video game site, which added to his involvement in cyberspace.

In 2007, Murdoch made the largest purchase of his life. He paid $5 billion for Dow Jones. The Bancroft family had owned the US publishing and financial information company for 105 years. The deal included the *Wall Street Journal*, an

Sharing His Wealth

In 1984, Murdoch was awarded the Companion of the Order of Australia for distinguished achievement in and service to the media and newspaper publishing to Australia and to humanity. Murdoch has made generous contributions to Australia's charitable, educational, cultural, and medical organizations. Murdoch's mother was granted the same award. In the United States, he has given considerable sums of money in support of political candidates and causes.

Murdoch's purchase of Dow Jones added yet more newspapers to the media tycoon's holdings.

international daily newspaper focused on business and finance. In the United States, it has the largest circulation of any newspaper, reaching more than 2 million readers.

The Dow Jones acquisition also gave Murdoch *Barron's Magazine*, MarketWatch.com, the *Far Eastern Economic Review*, and *SmartMoney* magazine. In addition, he received two radio shows: *The Wall Street Journal Report* and *The Dow Jones Report*.

WORLDWIDE INFLUENCE

Murdoch's accomplishments go far beyond the growth of one of the largest companies in the world and revolutionizing journalism. He has also changed the television and film industries. His powerful position and his control of a large segment of the media have given him significant influence in international industry, politics, and economics.

Murdoch's influence extends to the world's economy. He has pushed for international trade agreements

---

Still Voicing Political Opinions

After becoming a US citizen, Murdoch maintained political clout in Australia. In April 2007, he met privately in New York City with Kevin Rudd, a candidate for prime minister of Australia. The *Sydney Morning Herald* reported on the meeting: "Political leaders have long believed one of the keys to electoral success was to have Mr. Murdoch on side."[3] Neither of them disclosed what they discussed. In October, Rudd was voted Australia's twenty-sixth prime minister.

In 2008, the *New York Post* endorsed Barack Obama for the upcoming US presidential election. The paper supported Obama because Murdoch wanted to prolong the race. That summer, Murdoch and Obama met to work out a disagreement. By the end of the meeting, Murdoch and Obama had come to a tentative truce. Obama won the presidential election in 2008. He continued to see Fox News as his adversary, and some Fox News opinion shows continued to criticize Obama. Murdoch's Fox News was a media powerhouse. He had enough influence to warrant meetings with political candidates in at least two countries. And people listen, regardless of whether they agree with Murdoch's beliefs.

and has spoken on the global economy at the World Economic Forum in Switzerland. At the 2009 meeting, he encouraged US President Barack Obama to make the United States more competitive by investing in students to invest in the nation's future. Murdoch is also a champion of causes—mostly conservative—which attracts a wide array of admirers as well as critics. In mid-August 2010, he garnered media attention in the United States and abroad for his generous donation to the Republican Party. Murdoch had donated $1 million in support of probusiness Republicans running in the upcoming November elections that year. The entrepreneur was doing his part to keep his interests supported by those in power.

No Signs of Stopping

Murdoch is an outstanding entrepreneur who has created a massive dynasty. He has been enjoying business success for decades. His enthusiasm and curiosity are what have driven him to the top, to create an empire that reaches people worldwide. Murdoch does not talk about retirement. Printed newspapers are still his passion, though he has tolerated online news. The future of Murdoch's company, News Corp., is unknown. Perhaps one of Murdoch's children will step in and follow their father's footsteps. Or perhaps it will someday be sold to the highest bidder, just as the Bancrofts sold Dow Jones.

For now, Murdoch shows no signs of stopping his work in communications. Just as he has done throughout his decades-long career, Murdoch continues to look for opportunities to add to his empire all over the world. Fox Broadcasting Network has been Murdoch's greatest success. For Murdoch, "success trumps all"—it is the most important thing.[4] And where there is success, there is money and power and influence—the things that energize Murdoch and keep him going.

Murdoch has left his mark on almost every facet of media. He has touched the world of television with popular Fox programs such as *American Idol* and *The Simpsons*. His film company boasts a nearly endless list of blockbusters, including *Titanic* and *Avatar*. In Australia, Murdoch owns more than 20 newspapers; in Great Britain he owns five. In the United States, News Corp. publishes the *New York Post*, the sixth-largest newspaper. The *Wall Street Journal* is an international newspaper in print and online.

It is published in the United States, Asia, and Europe. In the United States alone, the *Wall Street Journal* has more than 2 million subscribers, which is the largest circulation of any US newspaper.

Murdoch is also in the book publishing business. His company owns Zondervan, a Christian book publisher, and HarperCollins, a publishing giant with more than 30 imprints spanning Britain, the United States, Canada, Australia, New Zealand, and India.

And the media giant's publishing ventures extend to the Internet, where his papers have online facets. In addition, he owns the social networking Web site MySpace and Imagine Games Network Entertainment, a multimedia company that focuses on gaming.

The media mogul loves what he does. Murdoch once described his passion for his work:

Heir Apparent

In July 2005, Lachlan Murdoch, oldest son of Rupert Murdoch, resigned suddenly from his executive positions at News Corp. The main reason, which the younger Murdoch had expressed to people close to him. was that Rupert had interfered in Lachlan's work and undermined him. Executives in the company reported, under anonymity, "Rupert and Lachlan had trouble maintaining a productive working relationship and as a result, their personal relationship suffered as well."[5] James, Lachlan's younger brother, is now viewed as the heir-apparent to their father's media empire. James is in charge of strategic and operational development of the television and newspaper productions in Europe, Asia, and the Middle East.

If you're in the media, particularly newspapers, you are in the thick of all the interesting things that are going on in a community. . . . I can't imagine any other life that one would want to dedicate oneself to.[6]

"Undoubtedly, when history is written Rupert Murdoch will be counted a giant. The question is whether he will be counted a visionary or a villain or both."[8]

—Ken Auletta, "Who's Afraid of Rupert Murdoch?"

Murdoch repeatedly says about News Corp., "We're change agents."[7] He has undeniably brought about change. Rupert Murdoch has revolutionized news and reshaped the world of journalism and the media.

Murdoch is the backbone of News Corp., and his success has left an undeniable mark on media worldwide, especially the United States.

TIMELINE

1931

Keith Rupert Murdoch is born on March 11 in Melbourne, Australia.

1950

Murdoch is admitted to Worcester College, Oxford University, in Great Britain.

1952

Murdoch inherits his father's newspaper business.

1963

Murdoch buys part of Asia Magazines Ltd.

1964

Murdoch buys the New Zealand newspaper *Dominion*, and he creates a new newspaper, the *Australian*.

1969

Murdoch owns controlling shares in Britain's *News of the World* and buys the *Sun*.

1955

Murdoch merges the *Sunday Mail* with rival newspaper the Sunday *Advertiser.*

1958

Murdoch buys television station Channel 9 in Adelaide and Sydney's *Daily Mirror* newspaper.

1962

Murdoch purchases Channel WIN 4 in Wollongong, New South Wales.

1969

Murdoch's interview by David Frost on *The David Frost Show* makes both men famous.

1973

Murdoch moves to San Antonio, Texas, where he buys three newspapers.

1974

Murdoch founds the *National Star.*

TIMELINE

1976	1979	1981
Murdoch buys the *New York Post*.	Murdoch buys controlling shares in United Telecasters Ltd. and Ansett Transport Industries.	Murdoch buys the London *Times* and *Sunday Times*.

1986	1989	2005
Murdoch creates Fox Inc. In October, Fox debuts its first program, *The Late Show*.	Fox launches *The Simpsons*, and Murdoch begins Sky (later BSkyB) television in Great Britain.	Murdoch buys MySpace and Imagine Games Network.

1982	**1984**	**1985**
Murdoch buys the *Boston Herald.*	Murdoch buys half interest in 20th Century Fox film studios.	Murdoch becomes a US citizen and buys the other half of 20th Century Fox films.

2007	**2009**	**2010**
Murdoch buys Dow Jones.	Murdoch announces he will start charging for online access to his newspapers.	In Britain, the *Times* and the *Sunday Times* start charging for online access to their content.

Essential Facts

Date of Birth

March 11, 1931

Place of Birth

Melbourne, Australia

Parents

Keith and Elisabeth Murdoch

Education

Geelong Grammar School; Worcester College, Oxford University

Marriages

Patricia Booker (1956–1965), Anna Torv (1967–1999),
Wendi Deng (m. 1999)

Children

With Patricia Booker: Prudence
With Anna Torv: Elisabeth, Lachlan, James
With Wendi Deng: Grace, Chloe

Career Highlights

In 1952, at the age of 21, Murdoch inherited his father's newspaper business. He began with a small Australian newspaper, the Adelaide *News*, and built an international media dynasty.

In 1969, Murdoch entered Great Britain's newspaper industry by
purchasing controlling shares in *News of the World* and buying the
Sun. In 1973, Murdoch moved to San Antonio, Texas, where he
purchased his first US newspapers. It was the beginning of US
purchases that would grow to include newspapers in New York City
and Boston, as well as the international publication the *Wall Street
Journal*. From 1984 to 2010, Murdoch built Fox, including the
purchase of 20th Century Fox film studios and the creation of Fox
Broadcasting Company, a fourth US television network.

SOCIETAL CONTRIBUTION

Murdoch's newspapers inform and influence, keeping readers
updated on current issues. His cable programs challenge viewers
to consider various viewpoints. His television offerings provide
entertainment. The long-running animated comedy *The Simpsons*
has become a cultural icon with such great influence that a lead
character's catch phrase "d'oh" has become part of leading English
dictionaries.

CONFLICTS

Throughout his business career, Murdoch has faced criticism
for his sensational journalism. In addition, some critics have
challenged his substantial media holdings, accusing him of
monopolizing media.

QUOTE

"If you're in the media, particularly newspapers, you are in the
thick of all the interesting things that are going on in a community.
. . . I can't imagine any other life that one would want to dedicate
oneself to."—*Rupert Murdoch*

GLOSSARY

altruistic
> Showing unselfish concern for others.

archrival
> Main competitor.

broadsheet
> A one-page newspaper with a large format, usually 15 by 24 inches (38 by 61 cm).

circulation
> The number of copies distributed of a newspaper or other publication.

conglomerate
> A large company made up of a number of smaller companies in diverse fields.

conservative
> Relating to a political philosophy of traditional views and values.

correspondent
> A person employed by a newspaper to report on a special subject or from another country.

editor
> The person who determines the final content of a newspaper.

journalism
> The profession or practice of reporting about, photographing, or editing news stories.

magnate
> A powerful or influential person in business or industry.

media
> The means of communication—for example, newspaper, television, and radio—that reach large numbers of people.

mentor
> A trusted adviser or teacher.

merger
> The combination of two or more companies into a single company.

mogul
> An important or powerful person.

national newspaper
> A newspaper distributed to an entire nation.

press
> The people and agencies that collect, publish, and distribute the news.

prime time
> The evening hours, usually between 7:00 p.m. and 11:00 p.m., when the largest audience is viewing television.

scandal
> A highly publicized incident that involves accusations of wrongdoing, disgrace, or moral outrage.

shares
> Equal portions into which the entire stock of a company is divided.

strike
> The refusal of employees to work or perform until certain demands are met.

subscriber
> A person who pays to receive a certain number of issues of a publication.

subsidiary
> A company completely controlled by another company.

tabloid
> A newspaper with a small format, usually 12 by 16 inches (30 by 40 cm), characterized by condensed, sensational news and photographs.

takeover
> A sudden and decisive change in control or management of a company, often by force.

union
> An organization of employees formed to bargain with the employer.

Additional Resources

Selected Bibliography

Leapman, Michael. *Arrogant Aussie: The Rupert Murdoch Story*. Secaucus, NJ: Stuart, 1985. Print.

Roberts, Johnnie L. "Murdoch, Ink." *Newsweek*. Harman Newsweek, 28 April 2008. Web.

Shawcross, William. *Murdoch: The Making of a Media Empire*. New York: Touchstone, 1997. Print.

Tuccille, Jerome. *Rupert Murdoch*. New York: Fine, 1989. Print.

Wolff, Michael. *The Man Who Owns the News: Inside the Secret World of Rupert Murdoch*. New York: Broadway Books, 2008. Print.

Wolff, Michael. "Rupert to Internet: It's War!" *Vanity Fair*. Condé Nast Digital, Nov. 2009. Web.

Further Readings

British Film Institute. *The Television History Book*. New York: Macmillan, 2008. Print.

Englart, Mindi. *Made in the USA—Newspapers*. Farmington Mills, MI: Blackbirch, 2001. Print.

Gitlin, Martin. *Joseph Pulitzer: Historic Newspaper Publisher*. Minneapolis, MN: Abdo, 2009. Print.

Goldsmith, Bonnie. *William Randolph Hearst: Newspaper Magnate*. Minneapolis, MN: Abdo, 2009. Print.

Roman, James. *From Daytime to Primetime: The History of American Television Programs*. Santa Barbara, CA: Greenwood, 2008. Print.

Web Links

To learn more about Rupert Murdoch and his media companies, visit ABDO Publishing Company online at **www.abdopublishing.com**. Web sites about Murdoch and his companies are featured on our Book Links page. These links are routinely monitored and updated to provide the most current information available.

Places to Visit

Dow Jones
1211 Avenue of the Americas, New York, NY 10036
www.dowjones.com
Offices of the US publishing and financial information firm and headquarters of the *Wall Street Journal*.

Fox Broadcasting Company
P.O. Box 900, Beverly Hills, CA 90213
www.fox.com
This is the home of the television studios where Fox prime-time television dramas and sitcoms are filmed. Audiences are not allowed for the filming of dramas, but Fox welcomes audiences for the filming of sitcoms.

20th Century Fox Studios
Century City, 10201 West Pico Boulevard, Los Angeles, CA 90064
310-369-1000
www.foxstudios.com
An extensive facility where a variety of genres are filmed, including full-length movies, sitcoms, commercials, and music videos.

Source Notes

Chapter 1. Becoming a US Citizen

1. David Gunzerath. "Rupert Murdoch." *Encyclopedia of Television.* 2nd ed. Vol. 1: A–C. Ed. Horace Newcomb. Chicago: Fitzroy Dearborn, 2004. 1559–1560. Print.

2. William Shawcross. *Murdoch: The Making of a Media Empire.* New York: Touchstone, 1997. 31. Print.

3. Richard Hack. *Clash of the Titans: How the Unbridled Ambition of Ted Turner and Rupert Murdoch Has Created Global Empires That Control What We Read and Watch.* Beverly Hills, CA: New Millennium, 2003. 220–221. Print.

4. William Shawcross. *Murdoch: The Making of a Media Empire.* New York: Touchstone, 1997. 219. Print.

5. Ibid. 215.

6. Ibid.

7. Ibid.

8. Jerome Tuccille. *Rupert Murdoch.* New York: Fine, 1989. 12. Print.

9. Ibid. 142.

Chapter 2. Young Rupert

1. William Shawcross. *Murdoch: The Making of a Media Empire.* New York: Touchstone, 1997. 19. Print.

2. Ibid.

3. Ibid. 27.

4. Ibid. 28.

5. Ibid.

6. Jerome Tuccille. *Rupert Murdoch.* New York: Fine, 1989. 10. Print.

7. William Shawcross. *Murdoch: The Making of a Media Empire.* New York: Touchstone, 1997. 57. Print.

8. Ibid. 32.

9. Michael Leapman. *Arrogant Aussie: The Rupert Murdoch Story.* Secaucus, NJ: Stuart, 1985. 21. Print.

10. William Shawcross. *Murdoch: The Making of a Media Empire.* New York: Touchstone, 1997. 37. Print.

Chapter 3. Beginnings of an Empire

1. William Shawcross. *Murdoch: The Making of a Media Empire*. New York: Touchstone, 1997. 45. Print.

2. Erin McWhirter. "Australia Celebrates 50 Years of Television." *Australian Associated Press*. News Limited, 5 Sept. 2006. Web. 19 Feb. 2010.

3. Richard Hack. *Clash of the Titans: How the Unbridled Ambition of Ted Turner and Rupert Murdoch Has Created Global Empires That Control What We Read and Watch*. Beverly Hills, CA: New Millennium, 2003. 74–75. Print.

4. Ibid.

5. William Shawcross. *Murdoch: The Making of a Media Empire*. New York: Touchstone, 1997. 50–51. Print.

6. Tom Shales, "Who's Afraid of Rupert Murdoch?" *Frontline*. Public Broadcasting Service, 1995. Web. 22 Aug. 2010.

Chapter 4. Expanding the Empire

1. William Shawcross. *Murdoch: The Making of a Media Empire*. New York: Touchstone, 1997. 58.

2. Ibid. 62.

3. Jerome Tuccille. *Rupert Murdoch*. New York: Fine, 1989. 23. Print.

4. Michael Wolff. *The Man Who Owns the News: Inside the Secret World of Rupert Murdoch*. New York: Broadway Books, 2008. 127. Print.

5. Ibid. 128.

6. Ibid. 130.

7. Ibid. 131.

8. "The McKay Kidnapping." *RachelScottJournalism.com*. Rachel Scott, 5 Feb. 2010. Web. 29 Aug. 2010.

9. Michael Wolff. *The Man Who Owns the News: Inside the Secret World of Rupert Murdoch*. New York: Broadway Books, 2008. 156. Print.

SOURCE NOTES CONTINUED

Chapter 5. Business in the United States

1. "Rupert Murdoch." *CBSNews.com*. CBS Interactive, 10 Feb. 2010. Web. 29 Aug. 2010.

2. William Shawcross. *Murdoch: The Making of a Media Empire*. New York: Touchstone, 1997. 105. Print.

3. Ibid. 105.

4. Ibid. 110.

5. "Just get Lost: it's Murdoch vs. Branson in the TV showdown." *Observer Online*. Guardian News and Media Limited, 4 Mar. 2007. Web. 22 Aug. 2010.

Chapter 6. Political Connections

1. Caroline E. Mayer. "Carter Staff , Murdoch Staunchly Deny Special Favors." *The Dispatch*. Google, 15 May 1980. Web. 10 Feb. 2010.

2. William Shawcross. *Murdoch: The Making of a Media Empire*. New York: Touchstone, 1997. 119. Print.

3. Ibid.

4. Ibid. 153.

5. Ibid. 160.

6. Peter Henderson. "Murdoch Yearns to Buy New York Times." *Reuters.com*. Thomson Reuters, 3 Sept. 2008. Web. 25 Feb. 2010.

Chapter 7. US Film and Television

1. William Shawcross. *Murdoch: The Making of a Media Empire*. New York: Touchstone, 1997. 187. Print.

2. Ibid. 226.

3. Tom Shales, "Who's Afraid of Rupert Murdoch?" *Frontline*. Public Broadcasting Service, 1995. Web. 22 Aug. 2010.

4. Michael Leapman. *Arrogant Aussie: The Rupert Murdoch Story*. Secaucus, NJ: Stuart, 1985. 271. Print.

5. Jerome Tuccille. *Rupert Murdoch*. New York: Fine, 1989. 136. Print.

6. Ibid. 7.

Chapter 8. The Birth of Fox

1. Kimmel, Daniel M. *The Fourth Network: How Fox Broke the Rules and Reinvented Television*. Chicago: Ivan R. Dee, 2004. 117. Print.

2. Richard Hack. *Clash of the Titans: How the Unbridled Ambition of Ted Turner and Rupert Murdoch Has Created Global Empires That Control What We Read and Watch*. Beverly Hills, CA: New Millennium, 2003. 9–10. Print.

Chapter 9. The Twenty-First Century

1. William Shawcross. *Murdoch: The Making of a Media Empire*. New York: Touchstone, 1997. 187. Print.

2. Esther Bintliff. "News of the World to charge for web content. *FT.com*. Financial Times, 18 Aug. 2010. Web. 31 Aug. 2010.

3. Alexa Moses and Kerry-Anne Walsh. "When Rudd Met Murdoch Subject Menu Was Secret." *Sydney Morning Herald Online*. Sydney Morning Herald, 22 Apr. 2007. Web. 18 Feb. 2010.

4. Owen Gibson. "How Murdoch Called Obama-Fox Truce." 3 Sept. 2008. *The Guardian*. Guardian News and Media, 3 Sept. 2008. Web. 18 Feb. 2010.

5. Richard Siklos. "Behind Murdoch Rift, a Media Dynasty Unhappy in Its Own Way." *NYTimes.com*. New York Times Company, 1 Aug. 2005. Web. 22 Aug. 2010.

6. Jerome Tuccille. *Rupert Murdoch*. New York: Donald I. Fine, Inc., 1989, 11. Print.

7. Michael Wolff. *The Man Who Owns the News: Inside the Secret World of Rupert Murdoch*. New York: Broadway, 2008, 2. Print.

8. Tom Shales, "Who's Afraid of Rupert Murdoch?" *Frontline*. Public Broadcasting Service, 1995. Web. 22 Aug. 2010.

INDEX

ABOUT THE AUTHOR

Sue Vander Hook has been writing books for 20 years. Although her writing career began with several nonfiction books for adults, Sue's main focus is nonfiction books for children and young adults. She especially enjoys writing about historical events and biographies of people who made a difference. Her published works include a high school curriculum and series on disease, technology, and sports. Sue lives with her family in Mankato, Minnesota.

PHOTO CREDITS

Peter Mathew/AP Images, cover, 3; Yvonne Hemsey/Getty Images, 6; Kirby Hamilton/iStockphoto, 10; iStockphoto, 13, 59; Craig Dingle/iStockphoto, 14, 96; AP Images, 17; TriggerPhoto/iStockphoto, 23; Jim Jurica/iStockphoto, 24, 97 (top); Keystone/Hulton Archive/Getty Images, 30; Aubrey Hart/Getty Images, 33; Hippo Studio/iStockphoto, 34; Anthony Baggett/iStockphoto, 37; Evening Standard/Getty Images, 45, 97 (bottom); Fotografia Basica/iStockphoto, 46; AP Images, 51, Photo by Bernard Gotfryd/Getty Images, 53; Charles Harrity/AP Images, 55, 56; Ira Schwarz/AP Images, 61; Anna Lubovedskaya/iStockphoto, 65; Ed Bailey/AP Images, 66; Ron Galella/WireImage/Getty Images, 71; Shannon Sweeney/AP Images, 73, 98 (top); 20th Century Fox /Photofest, 74; Twentieth Century-Fox Film Corporation/Photofest, 78; Richard Drew/AP Images, 81; Gino Domenico/AP Images, 83; Grace Studio, Tom Rollo/AP Images, 84, 98 (bottom); Mel Evans, File/AP Images, 89, 99; Bryan Charlton/AP Images, 95